NUGGETS OF TRUTH

Golden principles for successful living

Steve A. Cole

Nuggets of Truth

Golden principles for successful living

First edition

ISBN 978-976-8230-85-0

Author: Steve A Cole

Email: steve_cole@lycos.com

Editor: Stacey Palmer

Producer: Joy A Simons Brown

Cover design: Bjorn Campbell

ACKNOWLEDGEMENT

Thank you God for giving me the insight throughout my many life experiences; Thank you, God, for giving me the inspiration and placing me in the right mindset to translate these experiences into a compilation of thoughts that connect me to those who will travel this journey with me – my **readers**. I thank my Mom for her unwavering love and guidance as my parent, which she did under the love and admonition of the Lord, and for having invested in me the rich life lessons in a way only she could give. Heartfelt thanks also goes to, my sweetheart, Deserine for her loving support and encouragement during the course of this project. Also, sincere gratitude is extended to my friend HRH for asking me if I wrote the book yet, when I didn't. Thanks to all my other friends and well-wishers who cheered me on, especially when I needed it most.

To My Dear Readers

While life teaches us many subtle but important lessons throughout our daily experiences, we can all agree that some lessons are more fundamentally important than others. This book will explore, what the author refers to as "nuggets of truths", which in his estimation are some fundamentally important principles that govern successful living. If, in life, these lessons were to escape our notice, we would certainly not have escaped the ill-fated blunders and mishaps **engendered** by our ignorance. To not know these little nuggets of truths would be analogous to a blind man walking a busy thorough way without a cane. There are some simple principles at work in our lives that govern how successful we are at making good in whatever we endeavor to achieve, and not knowing *them* can equally assure failure. One wise one says "It takes a wise man to learn from his experience (good or bad) but an even wiser man to learn from the experiences of others".

It is my hope that you would have been counted wiser for having made the decision to read this book and grasp the gems that it entails; which will ultimately make your own journey a treasured experience.

Here is to giving yourself a fair shot at empowerment through the application of these principles in your life.

Cheers!

Steve

INTRODUCTION

Being an underdog for a long time can either break or make a man's spirit and his will and desire for living causing him to settle with just surviving. I've been there long enough to stop and wonder why the grass always looked greener on the other side. I've paused to wonder how my grass appeared to the person on the other side. From this, I was inspired to stop paying attention to others, but instead, make my own grass look greener to me.

While observing some major players in our global community, it becomes abundantly clear that with success, the level of importance that is placed on some things must be categorized: Some things are of importance, while others are of fundamental importance. For this purpose, let's make the distinction between important and fundamental importance, using the subject of a house, to amplify the point being made. We would agree that windows on a house are structurally important because, without it, we lose some functions that would bring much value to the house. Then, with the same logic, I am positive that you would be inclined to agree with me that the corner stone of that same house is fundamentally important. Why? Simply because removing those cornerstones would make the house into rubble. Without the cornerstones we have no use for windows either. In essence, we deduce that fundamental importance is the essential activity we must employ to assure success; but in the same vein, if neglected, almost guarantees the opposite.

For instance, a new company to the automobile industry could not be considered remotely competitive if it entered with manual handled windows in an industry where automatic powered features are the basic entry level requirement.... quite a laugh if you can imagine it! Right? Similarly, as individuals, we ought to make it our duty to understand the world in which we live and the principles at work in our lives. It is also equally important for us to employ them in ways that promote our personal goals to enjoy successful living.

In my quiet time, I often ask myself how I want to be remembered ...what will be my legacy? The thing about that question was that it inferred that I'd actually be remembered. The question actually confronts us indirectly with the reality that one day we will no longer walk the face of this earth, and the only thing about us that will be alive is our legacy. But there is no denying that some of us still sing Rod Stewart's forever young song in the back of our cerebral cortex somewhere just simply denying what will inevitably be all our fate. The thought is a tad morbid, I know, but here is something to be cheerful about...

The truth is if we were to accomplish what we would believe to be our truest human potential in our lifetime, we might not be so squeamish about meeting our Maker. For many of us, even though life gets difficult, we still aren't ready to die, because there is still so much we want to achieve.

The good news, however, is that once there is life, there is hope. So how do we achieve our truest human potential? At the end of the next couple of chapters, I will have offered clarity and shared with you helpful ways that will improve your life and ensure that tomorrow a brighter tomorrow awaits you on the other side of today.

Steve

Contents

NUGGET# 1

TIME WAITS FOR NO MAN

If all things were equal, meaning, if everyone was presented with the same opportunities in life - we all had the same financial start, no favoritism, no political bias, no discrimination... how would we end up? Would we end up being prosperous?

Now that you have paused and given it some thought, what is your answer? Are you satisfied with your answer?

I'm inclined to agree with you if your answer was no. That is because I've seen many cases where persons from destitute and impoverished beginnings, who have worked their way to wealth beyond many of their wildest dreams to become the savior of a generation that was destined for ill fate. I've far too many times seen youths who were born with the proverbial gold spoon in their mouths, yet have their stories told with a very sad ending. I have also seen individuals who have made tremendous strides in life to become successful, only to end up losing it all. The interesting thing is that their story didn't end there as they, like the mythical phoenix, rise again from the ash; and for them, such a misfortune was only a setback.

Suppose I told you that, although not apparent to us all,

we have all been somewhat granted a level playing field? You would all think that I was joking – that I have no idea of which I speak. Well, I'm not joshing you at all. Do you REALLY want to know the secret? Good! Now that I have your undivided attention, I'll tell you. I hope you are ready for this:

We get the same amount of time each day. Yes, it was really that simple. Every individual has been blessed with 24 hours in a day. Now, what we each do with those 24 hours is entirely up to each of us!

Time is that gift to us which is ever so precious. Simply because once lost, it can never be recovered. While I must say that it took me a while to learn, I have now learned that lesson. You see, when I was much younger and living with my mom she would give me several tasks to do around the house. This was her way of teaching me the important lesson of responsibility as well as the value of earning my keep. Well, that didn't always go down too well with me, as I had my own agenda which didn't particularly align with hers. I took my own sweet time to get around to completing my "chores". To cut a long story short, she would end up muttering some proverb about procrastination being the thief of all time. I didn't have a clue what she was talking about. She used this proverb to say that I was wasting my time if I keep delaying something that must be done, instead of doing it today. I later learned Edward Young (1683–1765), a British poet, was the first one who was credited to have said this.

Looking back, I often wished I had learned that lesson sooner. Now, though, I understand why they say, "Hindsight vision is 20/20".

I would have done a lot more in my early years had I known better then. What I have come to find is that those who know this simple fact DO more. And it is the 'more' that they DO that causes them to achieve more. When we procrastinate, we replace high-priority actions with tasks of low-priority, putting off important tasks for a later time. Some psychologists cite such behavior as a mechanism for coping with the anxiety associated with starting or completing any task. Go figure, I'm no psychologist, so I will offer no opinions in this regard.

Please bear with me as I go back to the story about my mom and me. Her planned home activities for me were no less anti-climatic and abrupt comparable to coitus interrupt us. A real disruption from my nirvana experience of chilling, lounging, watching TV, listen to music, did I say chilling? Oh yeah, and chilling. I got absolutely NOTHING done. But mom is a true life saver, because had I remained on that path, I would be absolutely NOWHERE today.

The trouble is there are many persons today stationed at nowhere wondering why no one ever told them this before they got there. That doesn't ever have to be you.

NUGGET # 2

TIME IS MONEY: UNIVERSAL CURRENCY

Because time is invaluable for every human being, one must exercise time management in every aspect of one's life. I often muse at the coined term "Time Management" though, because in reality we cannot manage or control time. So it really boils down to "self-management" or "self-control". The measure of time is unchanging and we are the only variable that can be controlled or managed. Time despite its unchanging nature, once lost, is lost forever. Although you might be lucky enough to be presented with other opportunities, the one missed opportunity that you got in a given moment will be lost. Putting things off robs us of the opportunity to accomplish something in the time that we sat around doing nothing. My time-lost experience has empowered me, as it has many others in generations past. While this is not a "how to" book, I will share with you a few little tips that I picked up along the way, that really helped me to master my use of time:

- Keep a To-Do list so that you can't "conveniently" forget about unpleasant or overwhelming tasks. It is called a "To-DO" list because what is placed on the list is to get DONE! You will have to DO to get it DONE!!

- Use an Urgent/Important Matrix to help prioritize your to-do list so that you can't try to kid yourself that it would be acceptable to put off doing something on the grounds that it's unimportant, or that you have more urgent things to be done, when, in reality, you are procrastinating. Just look up the "urgent important matrix" in a popular search engine online to learn more about this useful tool made popular by Dr. Stephen Covey.

- Become a master of scheduling and project planning, so that you know when to start those all-important projects.

- Set yourself time-bound goals; that way, you'll have no time for procrastination!

- Focus on one task at a time.

I won't be focusing on the how to, because if you understand why it is so important to change your thinking, it will ultimately result in the successful transitioning of it to your reality.

It is going to be the significant shift in your attitude that will determine the altitude you want to reach. You will come to learn the liberty in mastering your use of time and profit from less stress, better decision making and problem solving. I'm sure you are probably saying to yourself "Hmmm...Where have I heard this before? I know I've heard this before somewhere". You are right, you probably have! What I am sharing with you is no breaking news of a new discovery. It just happens to be an undeniable truth which we must embrace if we expect to be more than an ordinary achiever in life.

At one stage of my life, I used to work in the capacity of a sound reinforcement engineer. That job took me all over the island of Jamaica to events with wide and varied descriptions. I went from weddings to conferences to luncheons to political party meetings. But one very memorable event, for me, was a book launch I had done where this master surgeon about age60 had written his first highly anticipated book in the field of open heart surgery. What grabbed my attention most about that experience, was not just the many accolades that were bestowed on him, but the vastness of his service to the field he contributed. Just before he came up to give his vote of thanks, this great doctor was introduced by one of his colleague also of high repute. In that moment, it felt like an hour went by as the gentleman listed the many activities and involvement that this doctor had been in, and done throughout his career. If that guy were to have keeled over and died right there, we would have instantly had about 20 job openings. It is as though he has lived 3 lives in one. And I asked myself then and there, "How one man could do so much?" The man had seemingly sat on every company board imaginable.

Right there and then, it became clearer to me that night, that there is in fact, a symbiotic relationship between time and wealth. Those who were better stewards of time are, generally, good stewards of wealth.

Now it was all becoming clear. There are many truths to the saying that time is money, and that was just the tip of the iceberg. I was on to something, and I figured once explored, I would have unearthed many of life's hidden treasures.

NUGGET# 3

SUCCESS: FOCUSED PREPARATION MEETS OPPORTUNITY

Have you ever heard of a story of somebody you know who knows somebody that has an uncle that won a big lottery jackpot and how they had been living large since they made it big? Then somehow, no one heard anything about him for a while and the next thing you hear is that he's broke! You then ask yourself, "How could that possibly be? What could he have possibly done that would cause him to be broke? How could he not have anything to show for it? How could he have been so careless?"

So is that broke uncle just simply not having a lucky break right now? Do you think that some guys just have all the luck, while others have none? Is life just one big gamble? Do we just throw the dice and play? Unfortunately for some of us, life is just a game of craps...literally and figuratively speaking.

I had an interesting experience in college that provides another theory on the topic. I arrived in class about 6:30am, as I often would, because I lived a good distance off campus and in those days the public transportation system was neither predictable nor reliable. So to avoid ever being late, I'd set out really early. Class didn't start until about 8:30am, so I either had time to cool off a bit and chill before starting the grueling sessions or catch up on my readings.

This fine day in particular, my classmate and esteemed colleague, Dealo, entered the classroom, rather un-characteristically, early too. He greeted me, "What's up man?" to which I responded, "Just chilling". Dealo pro-ceeded right into a snap retort,

"That means you finished the homework due to be handed in this morning!"I paused, "What homework?" I had totally forgotten the Communications homework which was due that same morning. Because I was busy juggling a few other subjects that one snuck right pass me. Dealo quickly handed me the question sheet and said, "You better get started if you know what's good for you".

That hour while I was there writing away, my friend Dealo was telling me how he stayed up the night before work-ing on the subject and how tired he was; notwithstand-ing the fact that he was proud he was able to put his shoulder to the proverbial wheel and pull off a fine job. As expected, the teacher came later that morning, and before starting the lesson of the day made her request for the papers to be submitted.

A week later the results for that assignment were out. Among the noisy crowd huddled around the board was my friend, Dealo, checking to see what score he had received for his torturous night-up, trying to finish his paper. I stood apart waiting for everyone to disburse. I could see Dealo's excited face as he shouted back at me, "Mi pass youth! Mi get a B grade! I'll check yours for you..." and he did. He then came over to me and said in a most confused tone "I can't understand how you get the same grade as me" I laughed and responded "Shouldn't you be celebrating with me?" Without asking me any questions about how I did I the simply said, "Some people just lucky" and stepped away. I never forgot that moment because I believed there was something to take away from it.

Dealo attributed my passing the test to pure luck; and in a sense, I don't blame him. I study best in the wee hours of the night in the comfort of my home.

Dealo, being a resident of the college dorm rooms, would not have had the opportunity to see the amount of consistent hours I put in, weekly, into understanding the principles of what I was taught. However, what has faulted my friend was his thinking, i.e. a good crash study (what we called swatting) would win me in. He probably felt he, himself, got lucky.

To be really successful at something, takes dedication, which is really a fancy word for hard work and determination. Of course, there will be challenges in getting stuff done in the demanding world with so many things competing to capture your time. The truth is, most of these things are probably more fun than the things you necessarily need to be doing right now. But as Robert Schuller once said, "Tough time never last, but tough people do!".

Talk about tough people, and Mohammed Ali readily comes to mind. Ali was considered as being the world's greatest heavy weight boxer of all times. I had once read an article from a website where they cited how Ali started his day with early morning runs at 5:30 am. He would stretch beforehand, and then would run six miles a day in army type-boots in under forty minutes. Ali made sure he ate a wholesome breakfast- all natural foods, orange juice, and plenty of water.

After he ran, he would perform an exercise routine, after which, he would go back home to get washed up. Ali then went to the gym at 12:30 pm for 3 hours. After the gym, he would get a massage, and then get washed up. Ali made sure he trained 6 days per week with one day off, during which time; he would relax and ease his body and mind.

I want to make a point here though, so I will share with you an experience from my life to bring that point across. Being the supervisor of an IT department exposes a person to many things. One of the many functions, in the duties assigned, is to select the complement of staff you will be working with, to expedite the mandate of the department which, in part and parcel, is to support the goals of the organization. So, this meant that I, from time to time, sat on a panel of interviewers to evaluate the candidates' suitability for the company. After doing this for a while, I couldn't help but notice that almost everyone, when asked to tell us a little about themselves, informed us of how much of a hard worker they were. The truth is, it can be argued that some of them were just telling us what they thought we wanted to hear in order to land the job. Let's say we give them all the benefit of the doubt - everybody is a hard worker; yet not everyone rises to the top.

Hard work is one thing but working smart is another. Indulge me for a moment, just for one minute. Try to come up with the names of three persons you know who are really successful at what they do. When you have done that, ask yourself "Are they specialists at what they do?"Yep. Usually most driven individuals are not only hard workers but focused and driven. What it is really is developing a plan of action which will be geared towards accomplishing what they want and actually proceeding with the planned actions. It's about aligning your behavior with your desire. Take for example you struggle with being overweight and the need to lose some pounds to avoid health issues. In order to do this, it would mean that you'd avoid food with high fat content food and start exercising more each day. Simply put, you must act accordingly to achieve desired goal. Remember the Mohammed Ali story earlier? He consistently did the same training daily until he became the best. There is no two ways about it, you have to be fo-cused!

There are so many examples in recent past that exempli-fies and personifies this theory of mine and give us solid examples from which to learn. We had Usain Bolt, Asafa Powell, Michael Jordan, Tiger Woods, Serena Williams and many more who excelled for many years. These people in the sporting arena demonstrated character where ambition meets self-discipline.

I wish I could tell you that this is it for these people who have enjoyed personal success in their life, but it is not that simple.

I'm afraid there is a wide cross section of influential fac-tors that create the climate for success. From here on, the only thing I can do is encourage you to go out and do what needs to be done. Never mind the outcome so much as what you can learn from the experience. Just do it, and don't be afraid to make mistakes. Un-derstanding the principles is not enough; you must also place them into actions if you want to achieve anything. If you can understand this, you will understand the point that I have been making: You could read a book about the art of swimming twenty times over and would still not be a swimmer. Unless you have actually gone in the wa-ter and sufficiently practiced, you would not be able to confidently say that you are a swimmer. A very smart and insightful person once said that fortune favors the bold. I'm sure you will agree that this is a rather profound statement. My own interpretation of that statement is that we tend to earn more when we step outside our comfort zone and dare to do more than what is convenient.

I love my mom dearly; after all, she was my care-giver who nurtured me into adulthood until I could stand on my own. As I alluded to earlier, I wasn't the sweetest or the most obedient kid, but she really loved me unconditionally. I learned a lot from her, even the unspoken lessons by virtue of the way she lived. My mom really loved God, family and just people in general. She worked at the hospital for over thirty years as a secretary, but she made sure her duties included helping the helpless, the marginalized, and the ones who spoke, but were not heard. I believed she achieved success at home, how she lived, time management, and in having winning perspectives on the world in general. However, she was by no means perfect, because I saw her fail in some

things too. My mom was averse to risk and really wouldn't dare to step out into any unknown. She would rather stick with "the evil" she knew than to cause any ripple in the pond if she didn't have to. Even if I tried to simplify inflation in order for her to understand that she was earning a negative growth on her money in the bank, she would still prefer for it to sit there because it was safe, as far as she was concerned. In her mind's eye, risking it in any business investment meant losing it. It didn't matter to her that the investment could also mean a possibility of gaining much higher returns that can provide a surplus.

She would rather hold on to the false feeling of security that the illusive profit of a bank statement provides. I am aware that many persons who might have the same mind - set as her, might have read this and said, "So what's wrong with that?!"   For some, there is nothing wrong with that, but for the purpose of succeeding and achieving the optimum, it is far more than just a matter of right and wrong. There continues to be a notion that we can only be a success or be a failure. The trouble with that thinking is that, like my mom, persons often become crippled with the fear of failure which inevitably prevents them from taking risks whether calculated or otherwise. It is in that fear that we end up not starting anything, because we worry about not making the right decision. Nine-time NHL MVP Wayne Gretzky said it best when he said, "You'll always miss one hundred percent of the shots you do not take".

The truth is, instead of viewing failure as something to be avoided, turn it into a "stepping-stone" on the path to success and gratification. I have never met any successful person who has never failed. We must see success and failure for what they truly are. They're not opposites, but instead, opposite sides of the same coin.

Dave was a young sales rep whose first day on the job selling toaster ovens was discombobulating because no one seemed to want to buy any from him. That same evening he went to the boss and told him he wished to change departments or quit. Expecting some sympathy, Dave was flabbergasted when the boss let out a gusty wind of laughter. Dave became livid because his boss took his career for a joke. The manager gave Dave a piercing look that seemed to cut right through him and said, "You think I got this far because of my good looks?" Before Dave could get another word in, the manager said, "You want to leave because a couple people to-day told you no...well, I'll let you know sonny I'm here because I heard a lot more no's than you!" By this time Dave was left with a blank look on his face. The manager opened the office door ushering Dave out and said, "See you in the morning kid, tomorrow is another day to win".

The more mistakes you make (and learn from them) is the more you become a master of the art of what you are doing. So as a sales person with an increased fail-ure rate, the more people who tell you "no," the closer you will get to ultimate success. In other words, the more people telling you "no" now, the more people will say "yes" in the long term. The good news is that that prin-ciple is real in all aspect of life and not limited to that demographic of people who are called on to employ it on the job.

The trouble with many of us is that we don't really ask for what we want. After life throws us so many curved balls, we tend to become timid in our response to the world around us. Not convinced? Check out the guy who didn't ask the girl out because he was afraid of be-ing rejected by her. Check out the girl who didn't do the exam because she was terrified she would fail. The system is so constructed to establish penalties for not succeeding, that the unspoken message is transmitted to all those who become a part of it. We are led to believe that learning is demonstrated by accomplishing the goal rather than that it is acquired from the possibilities of mistakes that is made on the way to accomplishment. So rather than the few that dare to push past the mark, many find themselves towing the line and trying not to make any ripples. Speaking of line - let me share an experience I had, with you:

I was waiting in line at the bank with my Uncle Ted hoping to do a transaction together on an account he had dormant for a while. Of course, we weren't even sure we were in the correct line to begin with. My genius of an uncle turned to me and instructed me to go to the teller promptly after she was finished with a customer. My immediate response to that suggestion was "Are you crazy? Do you want the crowd in this long line become ticked off because you couldn't wait your turn?" my uncle just blankly looked at me and said in the most "matter of fact" tone, "Would you prefer we wait two hours to be told you need to join another long line all because we didn't ask?" I was crushed inside because deep down, I knew he had a sound point but my fear of being verbally abused from strangers was imminently more powerful than I cared to admit at the time. Before I could even utter a response, the buzzer went off indicating that the next teller was now available. Uncle Ted quickly stepped up to the lady who was next in line and interrupted her stride by placing his hand gently on her shoulder and said, "Do you mind if I could just quickly ask this teller a question before you transact?" By this time, I was right behind Ted to hear "Sure, go right ahead". I was flabbergasted! That's it? No one else said a thing and Ted and I just stepped right to the teller. Sure enough we were in the wrong line and the teller was kind enough to, not only point us to the right line, but also asked that we step to the side of an unoccupied booth where one of her colleagues would come to assist us so we wouldn't have to join another line. WOW! We were out in minutes, and I nearly had us wait for hours all because I was afraid to ask for what I wanted. That incident, though simple, highlights the fact that life usually rewards us for taking that one risk.

That lesson stuck with me to this day; a lesson that is biblical in natural –a principle that has been taught to Christians since before Christ. All we need to do was knock, and the door will be open to us. Ask and it will be given. Yet, somehow, this concept is seemingly foreign to many of us and absent from our daily living and surprisingly enough even some Christians. It later dawned on me why my grass never looked as green as the next man's own. I had been short-changing myself all those years because of my insecurities and low self-worth. I was grappling with my issues and being too concerned about what others thought, which created a strong sense of self-doubt.

Now that I think about it, this sense of self-doubt goes back as far as my diploma college years and maybe this very thing crippled my growth potential in my career. I had a college friend, Wayne, boarding in the house next to the one in which I lived. We used to travel the bus together since we attended the same school. Wayne was doing surveying at the building construction department and I was studying electronics engineering at the time. I recalled having a conversation with Wayne one day about job prospecting since we would soon be on the hunt. Wayne announced that he wouldn't be accepting any job that paid below seventy thousand dollars per year. Now for the early 1990's that was really good money to be paid in Jamaica. In that moment, I remember thinking that he must be nuts thinking he could actually ask for and receive that amount of pay.

Sheepishly, I did not even volunteer what my expectations were because they were way below his. As far as I was concerned, I was thinking realistically, because I could get by on thirty thousand dollars per year while I build my experience and work hard to become more skilled in my career of choice. Guessed what happened next? Wayne got a job in a few months forJ$72000 per annum, while I was still hunting and months later I landed an offer for $17,492.36 per annum with low fringe benefits and guess what happened next? I took it! Subsequent to that, I found myself going from job to job trying to earn what I valued. Unlike Wayne who obviously knew his worth, I had been selling myself short for years

and didn't know it. The system was simply responding to
that which I projected all because I was afraid to ask for
what I really wanted.

NUGGET # 4

CHANGE BRINGS NEW OPPORTUNITIES

So what happens when life happens to you? Do you take it standing up or bear it lying down? Do you try to get back up or wait to have someone help you up?

Experience is the hardest teacher. In the classroom you get the lessons then the test, but in life's experience we get the test first and are then forced to learn from it. Do we choose to react to any given situation or do we choose to respond? What determines our happiness?

As the word itself implies, happiness is associated with happenings, happenstance, luck, and fortune. If circumstances are favorable, you are happy; if not, you're unhappy. Yep, it's really true to our daily experience. Check this out...how do you usually feel when you get that paycheck at the end of the fortnight/month? Really good, right? A hard day's work for a day's pay. And how do you feel when the bills start rolling in, and you have to start paying out? Not so ecstatic any more. Right?

Now picture yourself waking up one morning before the alarm. You got a good night's rest, because the work load yesterday was light and the pressures were off because the boss went off playing golf. It's summer; the sun is out and shining in all its glory, and you really didn't have to rush because the kids are on summer break. What a great morning. You've had your fill of your spouse's best cooked meal which happens to be your favorite. Now it's off to work, so far so good with no traffic in sight. The day just simply could not get any better than this, and you love it. Your stop sign ahead goes red and you graciously come to a halt and then BAM! To the rear of your vehicle, there is a fender bender. When you check your rear view mirror, you see that it's an old lady sitting in a Buick who slammed into the back of your car. You come out arguing how on heavens name she could not have seen you stop, because the light was on red. To add insult to injury, she starts being rude to you for stopping without sufficient notice. You decide to exchange information, when you realize she isn't even licensed to drive because her license expired last year. In the blink of an eye, your day, which could not have been any better, just simply gets worst as every minute ticks away. Inconvenience and expense is now on the horizon which just messes up your flow, as you, like everyone else, are a creature of habit.

For so many of us, we can relate to this episode in some way, shape or form. Now let's analyze it for a moment and try to pick some lessons out of this, if we can.

The day is a beautiful day, and up to the time of that accident the day was still a beautiful day. So what changed? In the series of events that occurred, many of us would interpret the situation in such a way that leaves us to believe we are just fresh out of luck. So now our mood changes and we are unhappy. But why are we having this conversation? Why is it so important for us to understand that our happiness is heavily influenced by our environment? Simple, it's important to recognize that the only thing that is constant in life is change.

After switching careers and entering into the world of information, it was very apparent to me that technology changes so swiftly and it is only those of us who manage to remain agile will be left standing. The one thing you could be reassured of, is that there is something new coming around the corner. I made it my duty to be kept abreast with market happenings to ensure that I remained marketable. Instinctively, I learnt that one of the most essential life skills a person can have is the ability to adapt to change. So then, we can describe an adaptive individual as one who is able to refocus the mind in new directions and make choices based on his or her desired outcomes. However, adapting to change is difficult for most people due to the fact that humans are creatures of habit; having to change our patterns and behaviors is frustrating and annoying and takes us out of our comfort zone. Case in point: Let us return to the little episode we started this chapter with. Things were going good until that fender bender took place. The trip to work was the driver's usual pattern (same route... habit) until the "little" disruption of his routine. How he responds to it is determined by how quickly he adapts. Let's face it, the one thing he cannot change is the fact that this accident took place, so he'll just have to deal with it. It is daily living situations like these and others like it that makes the serenity prayer by theologian Reinhold Niebuhr (1892-1971) so well known even today. The words, though simple, are very effective....:

"God, grant me the serenity

To accept the things I cannot change,

Courage to change the things I can

And wisdom to know the difference.

Living one day at a time,

Enjoying one moment at a time,

Accepting hardships as a pathway to peace,

Taking, as Jesus did,

This sinful world as it is,

Not as I would have it,

Trusting that He will make all things right,

If I surrender to His will,

That I may be reasonably happy in this life,

And supremely happy with Him forever in the next.

Amen."

This is, indeed, a very powerful and potent message, which has been used to bring others to a closer reality of an elusive chase of happiness. Although many of us merely react to life, it is evident that it is more beneficial for us to respond soberly to the challenges that we are faced with on a daily basis. So after all that has been said in this chapter, what might our 'take away' be? I want to offer a few qualified observations. When we are confronted with unforeseen changes in our lives, our first response may be to either run away from it or fight against it. However, there are steps we can take to gain control of our fear, embrace the challenge and turn adversity into an avenue for success. Our attitude makes all the difference when dealing with adversity. Train the mind to see the change as a way to make something positive happen. This means we should think positively! We control how we think about and perceive changes. The more positively we think about change, the more positive our reaction to it will be.

Additionally, take time to analyze situations thoroughly. Think about the consequences of dealing with a situation in various ways. Ask, "What will I lose?" and "What will I gain?" "How could this choice affect my family, friends, self, and future well-being?"Also, view actions and circumstances from different angles and perspectives to gain an accurate understanding of what has happened. Further, we should communicate our concerns and ask questions to get information that might not be apparent. This will allow us to make informed choices. Finally, be willing to step outside of your comfort zone...it may prove to be a great experience. That fender bender could be a great opportunity for the man to help the elderly woman with a need she may have... could be a pair of glasses... you just never know ...an enriching relationship could have been borne from that single encounter.

NUGGET # 5

THE JOY IN CONTENTMENT

Growing up in the 'system', we have been oriented to think a certain way without even knowing it. It's as though we were programmed to operate a certain way so much, that stepping outside of those parameters would make us an anomaly within the matrix. If you have seen any of the matrix trilogy movies, you would immediately grasp what I have just said by that one line. For the others of us who might not have seen it yet, it is a movie that metaphorically emphasizes the conspiracy of a world system which we interact in but are often unaware of. Just for a moment, think back on how you were raised. Were you encouraged to get good grades in school? That way maybe we will get something on prize-giving day or enjoy graduation if you did well. If you stay in line and work hard, maybe you will be the one to get the employee of the year award this year. You never know. Maybe if the boss noticed that you have finished three (3) big projects this year within budget and on time, you will be up for promotion.

Notice that we have been oriented to laud and applaud only the big achievements in life. You are congratulated for graduating from school, for landing the big job, for getting married, for having a child, and so on. This is why persons are generally afraid to make mistakes because they don't want to mess up their chances for the next big thing. It is only the few empowered ones who realize it is ok to make mistakes.

If we mark our success as a destination and not as a journey - something to aspire to - we would have lost out on a lot of cool stuff on the way. In essence, what I am saying is small miracles happen every day; we just happen to miss out on noticing them, because we become so goal- driven and not process oriented. I recall seeing a forwarded email once with the usual positive messages. I gave it a cursory glance and one line popped out at me that I, since, haven't forgotten. It purported that a happy man is one who enjoys the scenery on a detour. It sure sounds a lot more refreshing than the usual ticked off feeling we get once we have recognized that we are either delayed or made late by an unannounced detour from our usual route that we planned our busy life to take on our way to the next meeting. I'm sure a lot more of us can identify more with the latter than the former situation.

To the core of all this, lies the notion of inner peace. Talk about inner peace and you can visualize yourself being unscathed by any random verbal diarrhea that escapes the lips of an angry motorist ranting from road rage. Ok, now that is quite a picture but you can frame that imagery in your mind around what is common to our urban experience today and contrast it with the joy that is not shaken because it resides deep within. I define that at the very core as joy, because it is not conditional to what is happening in a person's surrounding. It is these very things doctors cannot explain in medicine, why praying people overcome tremendous odds that may be stacked against them and seemingly have no trouble smiling at the storm. They cause people to leave their presence feeling blessed rather than depressed at the end of a visit.

Usually persons like these have a deep awareness and reverence for their God. Evidently, for most, this joy is posited to be directly related to God and is the firm confidence that all is well, regardless of ones circumstances. You should be joyful when you encounter various trials because trials produce spiritual and emotional endurance and maturity. In essence, before you quip to ask "why did God allow this to happen to me?" try considering this truth for a minute: God is far more interested in your character than he is in your comfort.

Interestingly enough, we naturally have this tendency to want to be self-sufficient and take care of all our needs, but adversity often culture a small reminder that having our lives interwoven with others is no accident. In as much as we can be blessed by others, we have the opportunity to be God's hand extended and bless up others too. In the search for happiness, the individual focuses upon himself or herself, but joy moves a person out of a self-centered preoccupation and provides an orientation towards others. Joy is an experience which connects us to that which is "greater" than we are. It connects us to the creative power that is more than the "I" or ego. Joy gets us out of ourselves and in contact with this "Other" and with others. Can we allow ourselves to find joy, or has that ability to feel joy been lost in the child we once were.

NUGGET # 6

THE GIFT OF GIVING

In so many ways I'm often impressed by kids. One such reason is the amazing way in which they effortlessly form friendships. It is the pondering of this reality that I have come to recognize the purity of a child's innocence as being precious. I say this, because it has become so obvious to me that who we are as adults arise from how we are cultured and what we learn by our experiences. That valuable commodity of innocence through time becomes eroded and corrupted by attributes learnt by our exposure to some harsh realities of this world. Some become hardened as a defense mechanism to shield them from life's ills and yet others of us learn greed, malice, envy and prejudice among other misgivings and hand me downs that, which in more cases than not, sadly come from our parents.

Speaking of defense mechanism, please allow me to digress a little to make a small point here. I always liked biology in school, and I didn't limit my studies to the science of human and social biology, but had an interest in the wider animal and plant kingdom. It was always an interesting phenomenon to me how there were so many threads of commonality between us and what we would describe as less intelligent beings relating to the environment we inhabit. Let's look at the stingray and octopus for a minute. The stingrays are a group of rays, which are cartilaginous fishes related to sharks. Most stingrays have one or more barbed stings on the tail, which is used exclusively in self-defense. The stinger may reach a length of approximately 35 cm, and its underside has two grooves with venomous glands. The flattened bodies of stingrays allow them to effectively conceal themselves in their environment. Stingrays do this by agitating thes and and hiding beneath it. Stingrays are usually very docile and curious. Nevertheless, the stingray's defensive reflex (use of its poisoned stinger) may result in serious injury or death. The Octopus, however, has numerous strategies for defending itself against predators, including the expulsion of ink, the use of camouflage and dalmatic displays, their ability to jet quickly through the water, and their ability to hide. Yet, what is most interesting is that al octopuses are venomous.

So what is the point I am making? The comparison between these two creatures of the sea is their difference in equipment as their God given tool for survival. For the stinger, if hiding doesn't work its next line of defense is to spur with its venomous stinger. While on the other hand, the Octopus, despite being venomous, will employ several tactics to elude its predator. This, of course, is because Octopuses are highly intelligent, likely more so than any other order of invertebrates. What is most interesting is that young octopuses learn almost no behaviors from their parents, with whom they have very little contact.

Humans, however, have a much more intricate adaptive intelligence system and, by contrast, learn much from our parents and the environment which we inhabit. But the beauty about how God constructs us can also be found in the ability to make choices. Like the stingray and the octopus, we have the ability to react to the environment around us but beyond the intelligence displayed by the octopus we can choose to respond than react to stimuli. It means, then, that we have this incredible ability to adapt to our environment that immensely increases our survival rate in the world around us. It means, also, that our intelligence avails us the opportunity to assess what action brings desired success and change our behavior to access that success in our many endeavors. That is why we hear the popular quote that it's insane to do the same thing over and over and expect a different result. Trust me; you need to be very upset if someone calls you a pea brain because I have witnessed a lizard fight himself swollen for hours before a mirror thinking he was going to win his opponent. We have been so blessed with an aptitude that permits us to identify with clarity the world around us and make it work to our favor.

Ok, so let us get back to what we can learn from kids having understood within the context that humans learn and adapt to survive in the environment they inhabit which pretty much dictates more so how we behave in adult years. But more importantly, I want to make the point that some skills we had as kids should never be abandoned. A very poignant example could be, when two kids meet in a park the magic starts and its play time. To them, they are just two kids in a park having fun. Where he is from, what school he attends, the color of the skin and the financial disposition of his/her parents don't matter...until one of their parents comes along and briskly whisks him/her away and tells him/her that they don't ever want to see them talking to that child again. What a message! Well, that is for a whole other book.

I'm making the case that there are some things we can really learn from kids that even in our adult life still has immense value today as it did when we were innocently on the playground easily making friends without judgment. In that newly found friendship when the children play, oh what fun it is to share toys. Looking back on my own childhood years, I was raised as an only child. For the most part I didn't know what it was like to have a sibling, so I didn't miss having a brother or a sister with whom to play. That being said, I did, however, find great value in the company of my cousins when we got together. Although I didn't have many toys, I was never short on toys. But from what I can remember, I didn't play with my toys a whole lot; at least not until I had someone with whom to play. In other words, my wealth of collections had little value until I had someone to draw my attention to them.

And so it is today, there is just a spread of happiness when we share what we have and the experiences we have with people. In its purest of intentions, sharing what we have is never about boasting about our collection of valued trinkets. Instead, it is the partaking of an experience or thing - it is where the lesson of equity begins.

In any event, I can only remember a good feeling when I was able to assist someone with what I contributed to their life by sharing what I have. I can only remember a good feeling when I was blessed by someone who shared what they had with me. In the same vein, I also remember the disappointment I felt when someone was selfish about what they had. I can recall the look of hurt on someone's face when I allowed greed to prevent me from sharing what I had. I also didn't forget the regret I felt knowing it wouldn't have made me any worse off for sharing what I had and the difference it would have made to that other life had I just shared. Plus, my conscience would have taken me for a ride if I didn't learn from the experience let alone make right the wrong, in some way, shape or form.

Imagine you had within your hand a rock. Imagine your fist tightly clenched around that rock so much so that no one can take that rock away from you. It is all yours and no one else can have it. But what if you were to open your hand and freely give that rock to someone. In the same way you might have blessed someone by giving that away, your hand is now free to receive a precious stone someone is prepared to bless you with.

Golden principles for successful living

NUGGET # 7

THE WORLD'S BEST INVESTMENT INSTRUMENT

Here is a reckless statement: "Capitalism is driven by greed". This bold declaration can be the catalyst for much debate. Greedy and self-centered behavior doesn't just affect others, as a matter of fact one could easily argue that the ones who suffer the greatest from selfish behavior, are the selfish people themselves. Self-centered people live cocooned, unhappy lives, never realizing that real happiness comes from loving, appreciating and understanding the people around them, and not from the things they possess or the people they control. Why did I start off on this note?

Well, I wanted to make one simple point on a matter that has come home to my consciousness over the years. It would seem that our culture in the western world have taken on commercialism as the character that drives who we are as a people; so much so that we keep buying in order to keep ourselves happy. It becomes so easy to fall into the cycle of thinking that the more we have, the happier we will be. But why would anyone think this? Because we have been sold so well by the marketers who tells us what our next move should be. The pride of life engages us into thinking that if we get that next thing we will be noticed, recognized, or sought after.

My cousin George (name changed to protect identity) just got this hot new red jag not so much because he has a need for speed or that he just loved the smell of the brand new leather interior that only a jag can give but because it makes him more attractive to the kind of ladies he wants to "take for a ride". Read between the lines if you must, but I figure you got the picture. So Suzie(name changed to protect identity) didn't just buy that J-Lo hipster jeans simply because she thinks it looks cute on her...even though that's what she told us. But way down in her subconscious she remembers seeing George checking her assets out as she walked by, and she has been dying for him to ask her out so maybe she could have him take her to see a movie in that new jag of his. Innately we buy more to acquire more, which ultimately makes us feel important. Acquisition of things, by design, has been staged to help us maintain the status quo or simply help us to keep up with the Joneses.

Marketers know this because they understand the psyche of people in terms of what drives us and work hard at "selling" us goods in a way that appeal to our five senses.. So subliminally, we learn to love things and use people. But ideally what will always work as intended for the good of all is for us to love people and use things. For far too long the world as we know it has warped this reality and shifted gears to an elusive dream for happiness. If we are not people-oriented, we will find ourselves searching for happiness in things to fill that void lost outside of the human connection.

The inescapable reality is that there is just a satisfaction that cannot be replaced when we touch another human life in a positive way. Simply put, by focusing on and investing in others, we can improve the world that we live in. Those who participate in charitable events, and who spend time learning and caring about people from all over the world, quickly realize how much they can gain personally from these selfless activities. Persons who do multi level network marketing would quickly appreciate the principle emphasized in this chapter because of the mentoring system they have structured where successful persons impart successful ways of the business for others to duplicate. This is a far contrast to what we see in many traditional corporate environments where people step in others neck and walk on their backs in order to get to the top.

NUGGET # 8

GREAT LEADERS = GREAT SERVANTS

Most young boys who dare to have a dream would someday dream to be the conqueror of their own world – to be called great. I was no different, and my own idea of great was conceived in the form of a king. I would harness great wealth and power and command the respects of those around me. It certainly wouldn't be too inappropriate for my loyal subjects to lavish me with my heart's desire. I would have what I want, when I want it and how I want it. Never mind the fact that I might want ice cream and chocolate cookies for dinner every single day.

But that was then and this is now. The awakening of my awareness to the world impacted my dream tremendously after making mental notes of the many things I observed. Evidently, history has a way of telling its story, your story and my story - and very well too. I have come to find that the men who are lauded as great among men are the ones who were willing to serve others. Take a look at Marcus Garvey who became convinced that uniting blacks was the only way to improve their condition. Additionally, take a look at Mohandas Gandhi who employed non-violent civil disobedience as an expatriate lawyer in South Africa, in the resident Indian community's struggle for civil rights. They gave their lives for a cause that was bigger than themselves to the aide o the human race.

Talk about greatness personified, and Jesus the Chris said it himself - that he did not come to be served but to serve and to give His life as a ransom for many. So, too we ought to learn from these men among men whom we call great.

"For my own Part, when I am employed in serving oth ers, I do not look upon myself as conferring favors, bu as paying debts. In my travels, and since my settlement I have received much kindness from men, to whom shall never have any opportunity of making the least di rect return, and numberless mercies from God, who i infinitely above being benefited by our services. Those kindnesses from men, I can therefore only return on thei fellow men, and I can only show my gratitude for these mercies from God, by a readiness to help his other chil dren and my brethren. For I do not think that thanks and compliments, though repeated weekly, can discharge our real obligations to each other, and much less those to our Creator." Letter to Joseph Huey (6 June 1753) published in Albert Henry Smyth, The Writings of Benja min Franklin, volume 3, p. 144.

I couldn't have said it better myself. I'll say no more on this...I'm certain you have gotten the point! Oh no...I' say one more thing. Take a look around; if you do no see anyone following, then you do not lead...you are simply taking a walk!

NUGGET # 9

IT ALL STARTS WITH AN IDEA

When I think about it, I laugh, but it sure must tick some parents off real good. Sometimes parents go out of their way to buy kids some most expensive and elaborate toy with bells and whistles but it somehow gets to the bottom of the toy pile only to be touched once or twice since it's been bought but alas, the kids can be found having a whale of a time with a piece of paper to simulate sounds of a motor vehicle playing at their leisure. Just amazing! The biggest asset a child has is the ability to dream...to create a world of his own using the power of the mind! Certainly, the most expensive toy doesn't necessarily do that.

It can be posited then, that the imagination is both a vehicle for human creativity and a vital social force which leads us. Don't believe me? Give a set of 8year old a set of lego and see what they make of it, given some time! Still not a believer?

So why do most of us adults never get it? Ok so you have your own theories...here's mine: It's because we've been cultured to quit playing and grow up. Nod your head up and down if you agree. If you don't, shake your head side to side. For far too long our system has caused us to view the word "play" as the negative and polar opposite of "work". Play is too often regarded as a euphemism for laziness, trivial activity, whereas work suggests serious, purposeful activity. This is not something taught in school through books; the messages are subliminal and powerful.

Do you remember your mom saying to you, "put those toys down and go take up your school book! You've played enough for one evening..." that sure puts a wedge between learning and fun doesn't it. It certainly gives the impression too that learning can't be fun. Not to mention the fact that it suggests that learning is highly improbable during play. So anyway, my real question is..."Are we going to charge sheep for bleating?" It's what they do, so why stress kids for playing. After all, play is the serious work of childhood.

Are you still nodding your heads? Good! I'm glad we're on the same page. Why, then, are so many of us willing to burn bridges between childhood and adulthood? Remember the lego?

The creative bridging starts with the mind. Every chair we sit on was conceived in someone's mind. The greatest bridges that join lands began with the seed of a thought. Therefore, it is safe to deduce that how our future looks is based on our own view of it and what we imagine it to be. Thus, the wealth in hand can be shaped by the wealth of knowledge we have which is based on the well-being of our minds. How well does your future look?

I grew up hearing the Chinese proverb that tells us that a journey of a thousand miles begins with a single step. I must admit that I liked the way it sounded and understood it when I first hear it. The emphasis was on the first step. Just start.

So you have a great idea...no wait, you have several great ideas...you could change the world with your inventions but alas you haven't started...and the world continues to spin. You've been doing great, or so you think, because you have spent the time creating your feasibility studies, swot analysis, market segmentation, and financial projections and compiling the business plan, draft the demo, made the prototype. All that work...wow... though all very necessary, have you really started doing business yet? Nope! You can't afford to rest until that first product is in the hand of a transacting customer.

Like most major cities of any country where there is a significant presence of poverty looming, there seems to be at almost every stoplight a beggar with their hand outstretched asking for money. At a particular stoplight in my hometown there usually stands this elderly woman who looked like she was in her eighties. She could possibly be younger in light of the fact that she appeared to be given very little care over an extended period. From all indications, she was at the same spot every morning, begging the occupants of every car that passed. I found myself thinking about what could have happened in her life that would have caused her to end up on the streets begging – what was her story? Where was her family, and why weren't they helping? Then, one day I saw her crocheting (the fine art of making fabric from thread) and I was flabbergasted at the sight of this woman with a skill worth its weight in gold; yet she was poor. Why?

It heavily dawned on me that her poverty began in the mind, just like so many of us. In Jamaica, crochet is a dying art. Even so, there were still people who would have been willing to pay thousands of dollars for clothing of all kinds as well as bed spread made or accented with crochet. This elderly lady had two valuable assets that could have earned her a fortune, had it been put to good use. Here she had time on her hands and a skill her still functioning hands had mastered. Yet she was begging for just enough to get by; mind you, this was my assessment of her situation.

How many of us are really like that? We are too lazy to work hard, so we do just enough to survive and get by. How many of us can honestly identify some God given talent with which we have been blessed and we have still not worked at maximizing on it to achieve our fullest human potential? What we do with the gifts we have been given is what makes the difference.

NUGGET # 10

CREATIVITY: THE INTELLIGENT SIDE OF PLAY

When I was a little boy it wasn't uncommon for me to dream on a regular basis. Some of those dreams were really fabulous too; talk about lifestyle of the rich and famous. I was living in mansions with many rooms and driving some of the hottest cars...until I woke up of course. But those dreams always left a smile on my face. Of course, the older I got, and the more socially conscious I became, the more detailed oriented the dreams were. The mansion construct was more defined, the rooms were no longer rooms but became more functionally detailed. I wanted a personal study room with my own library. Then there was the gym to keep me buffed. Also, there was the entertainment room with the plasma screen and surround sound for my own viewing and listening pleasure. Oh and about the rides, I now had company...good looking company. Naturally, you understand that she would have been the Miss Universe of the day.

Sounds great, right? But here is the crazy part: it hadn't really occurred to me in those days what would be the vehicle used for realizing this dream. For me it was all a fantasy, an escape to the world of the haves and away from my reality of have not. It could never be too soon for me to now ponder how I was to make this fantasy an everyday reality.

So anyway, fast forward about seven jobs and three careers later, I pondered my circumstances. I realized, at the time, that my reality was still afar way off from my dreams. Interestingly, the jobs I had over the years had taken me as far as the east is from the west in making the dreams real in my everyday experience. After spending some real quality time to do some self-examination it came home forcefully that over time life pushed me around like it did everyone else. And I seemed to have responded like most everyone else...I took it. The many disappointments had shaped my thinking to not expect much and by extension caused me not to demand much of life. So when the big dreams came square with the salary earned the dream was shrunk to fit the reality of a less than fabulous wage to establish comfort in what I thought then to be a justly rewarded pay. Consequently, I said "Bye-bye" to the mansion with ten cars and hello to my two bedroom town house with family minivan; here I come. I dreamt less, so the many business ideas I had shelved in the corner of my mind never got much chance to come out and play.

I could have contributed much more to my environment had I simply played with some of my ideas. What an injustice I have served on both myself and society having sacrificed toying around with some of my ideas. After all, the chair we sit on was someone else's idea and so too, the building we work in. They were simply well thought out and constructed with coordinated activities to make it happen.

Things were different, because I had a new burst of energy which stemmed from a resurgence of passion I had buried a long time ago. Now I was determined to find the next big thing that would surely impact society. I searched my thoughts and looked around me for ideas to fill an unmet need. Certainly, I was to create my own niche market, I thought. If you are rolling on the ground with laughter by these few lines of thoughts I've shared with you, it would mean that you have certainly been there and done that.

For the rest of you young bloods who thought that was a genius of an idea, draw close and hear this...utter rubbish!

After wasting much of my time on that quest, it dawned on me that there is absolutely nothing new under the sun. A clear example of this being evidenced is the fashion industry where styles are recycled almost every decade. Yes, yes, yes I know what the younger ones are going to tell me now. You have to be decades old to notice, but for all intent and purposes please accept my word on this one. Believe me, the best thing to do is find an area you love and either do it differently from others or simply do it better than others. Let the signature of your work be the uniqueness that appeals to consumers and keep them coming back to do business with you.

NUGGET # 11

HELPING OTHERS WIN MAKES YOU A WINNER

I like to see people succeed. In truth, it impresses me when someone fights against major adversities and wins. That's one of the many characteristics that attracted me to my wife. That is not to say that it escaped my notice how beautiful and intelligent she is. She seems to not be deterred from accomplishing her goals no matter the setbacks that might come her way. I find that kind of tenacity an endearing attribute that is to be commended. There is such a warm and fuzzy feeling you get inside when you look upon the courageous who dared to be and do differently having pressed on against all odds to come out triumphant. As you read on you are probably nodding your head in affirmation right now to this expressed sentiment. That is, if you aren't what the streets call a "hater". The reason you agree is because deep down we know that this kind of brass isn't so common. Ok, let us check the temperature on that statement. How many times have you either seen someone who has been through a lot of crap life throws them or watched a movie character passing through one adversity after another and then say to yourself, "Darn! If that were me I'd have quit long ago". A few times? Once or twice? Can't count? It's easy to give up or to put it nicely, and say that we can't be bothered. For this very reason, some people will cheer for and/or sympathize with anyone who must overcome incredible feats in their lives.

Case in point:"The Pursuit of Happiness" is a 2006 American biographical drama film based on Chris Gardner's nearly one-year struggle with homelessness. This movie, because of its relatable content, hit the box office as a smash. Even to this day, because of what it does and what it represented, people refer to this movie which speaks to the strength of the human spirit. Everybody loves to see the underdog turn out to be the top dog. That's the very reason "the karate kid" is such a classic movie to this day.

I promise you, if you view the world as though it is giving you a fight, it will definitely give you that. How you perceive the world and yourself greatly affects how the world receives you and treats you. Stop thinking that it is you against the world! Generally speaking, many people want to see others succeed. People want to see you reach your fullest human potential.

People are our most important resources and also a great source of our prosperity. Remember what I said earlier though, it is not that we are to use people and love things as the world standard currently has it; but, instead, we are to love people and use things. I want you to recognize that we are not an island and so we should dare not stand alone. The spirit of community raises the awareness of singleness in purpose for the greater good of the community. No one really cares about what we have to say to them unless they know that we actually care about their welfare.

When we create the way for others to see a better way out for themselves, we have done much to empower the individuals. True success happens when you "pay it forward" – help someone else after you have been helped or have succeeded. It is so important to help others to win. We need to believe in people before they succeed. What you make happen for others, will eventually come back to you; rest assured that someone will be there to help make it happen for you.

I will hasten to instruct you not to help others just because you view it as investment from which you should expect returns. Giving is oftentimes a thankless job and so the focus should be on helping to meet a need in someone else's life to make them the better for having done so From this, God will richly bless you. Don't look for thanks or a pat on the shoulder for well doing.

I will repeat for this is most important not to miss: do not ever make the mistake of waiting for a thanks or looking for a pat on the back to tell you a job well done. That is a breeding ground for self-righteousness which endangers the giver to harbor thoughts of him/her being a better person than others for having done the good deed.

Like I said before, people won't care what you have to say unless they think you care. So without saying too much on this, it is to your benefit to understand the fundamental principles of human behavior to influence and by extension achieving results through others. Of course this requires you to be an excellent communicator as well. Earlier I was encouraging us to use things and love people; in that same vein we should then be managing things and leading people. Let us be clear, though, that leading people is not telling people what to do, but helping others to take charge, which will happen if you first help them to identify the potential in themselves.

Helping others to believe in themselves and that they are capable of achieving more goes a long way when you can successfully tie in their motivator to achieving their idea, dream and goal. This will harness a culture of building a community with a singular focus to developing a goal. People feel good participating in a higher purpose and it will be your job to effectively articulate this purpose. Remember now, they already want to see you succeed as much as they desire it for themselves.

NUGGET # 12

IT COSTS YOU NOTHING TO CHANGE YOUR MIND

Lifelong learning is the continuous building of skills and knowledge throughout the life of an individual. It occurs through experiences encountered in the course of a lifetime – experiences that you will never be short on. Whether you learnt the lessons in life out of your experiences early or not, will determine just how pleasant or not so pleasant most your experiences will be. Although that one line may sound somewhat abstract to some, the message behind it is that there lies within all that is a bit of good news.

First off, you don't have to spend your whole life trying to learn some lessons. The other good news is that putting into practice the lessons you have learnt throughout your life translates to a much higher probability of an enriched life experience. The converse is true; that ignorance of these fundamental truths we have discussed in this book can cause us worrisome experiences of not being able to grasp opportunities that may come our way. Life doesn't have to be a game of chance where a pay load is a lucky draw and negative cycles are considered bouts of bad luck. We can achieve what we desire out of life by not just simply working hard but by applying a focused effort toward our goals.

It is evidenced from the litany of examples abound that engaging in this focused effort to accomplish ambitions requires self-discipline. You have learnt that it is important that you be bold about your choices and stand by them. There will be a whole lot more nay-sayers than there will be cheer leaders in your corner. Do not be daunted by this reality but embrace and feel empowered by it. None of the persons who are revered as 'successful' today, ever went throughout their entire life without strong oppositions. In fact, you will need to learn to toughen the inner man and persevere because, at some point, you must trod through a bunch of 'no's before you get to a 'yes'. That is why it is so important that we never fear failure. But it is important to note that you can only embrace failure if you seek the lesson to be learnt from it to take you to the path of success.

So don't be shy about asking for what you want. You just might get it. Though not explicitly defined in this book, you would have learnt that emotional intelligence is necessary for wholesome living, because our happiness is greatly influenced by our external environment which changes unpredictably like the weather. It is for this reason that we must strengthen the inner man with peace and joy with God in the center so that no matter your circumstances in the present, you remain resolute that your future can be filled with bright possibilities. That, my friend, is the shaping of your fate through the exercise of your faith.

When you can appreciate how beautiful life can be

when living by faith, you can't help but want to share this with others. It is for that very reason why I have taken the time out to share my insight with you by writing this book. There is enough happiness to go around for every-one if everyone is willing to share what, and who makes them happy to begin with. So if a life in God makes you happy why, would you want to keep Him to yourself? Although more times than not it's hard to explain what seems illogical at the surface.

Just go try it and you will see that I am right. Go invest in others by just simply giving, and you will see, intrinsi-cally, that you are giving to yourself each step of the way. This book is not a 'how to' book, but if you don't practice the principle imparted you simply won't get it. Go share, go and invest in others, go give, go and serve! History will be kind to you for having done so. I don't want to leave you hanging in my departure from the journey that is this book, without putting all that I have said into perspective. The self-discipline I had alluded to earlier really means that having this new view on life is simply not enough. To have a change of mind is the first of many steps leading to a change of life style. You will have to have a change of habits. Remember now that your habits are learnt behavior that you do without even thinking about it. You have done it so much that it has become second nature. So what we want to do here is to kick the bad habits we have formed to the curb so they no longer keep us from achieving our highest hu-man potential that God has designed for us.

Your habits, whether good or bad, will greatly deter-mine your future! If you keep doing what you have al-ways done you will always get the same result. So, it is necessary to evaluate what has not been working, and change it. You must start by consciously changing your everyday habits, but you must first identify what are some of the unhealthy practices you have been sub-consciously doing that go against your desired goal and transformation in your life. Kicking these habits will require that you start doing the things that align to your life goals and shun those activities that do not.

Yeah, I hear you muttering the words "Easier said than done" in the back of your throat, and you are right. So it means you not only have to have the passion for posi-tive change in your life but will now have to use that pas-sion to drive the behavioral change to create a routine in your life that will give you the result you want. Now, I am not trying to target persons who suffer from obesity, but I know that it is clearly understood of which I speak. If they want to be back to a weight that is reasonable to their proportionate height, they will now have to devel-op a routine of exercise (good habit) that will help them lose weight. Not only that, but such a person will have to kick the habit of late night snacking and other similar behaviors that oppose the goal in mind. So again, I am simply saying that we will have to align our passions with behaviors that create habits that align with our goals.

Please, please, I beg of you, don't just read this book for reading sake. If you fail to assert some of these attributes (provided you might not have already done so) to your own life experience then beyond reading this book, the book would have served better as a paper weight supporting a crooked lamp that nobody uses, because it's just there for the decor. My hope for you is that you assimilate the knowledge transfer to your life to make it enriched.

Your next step is to translate these ideas into your reality by choosing to change the way you perceive the world around you and appropriately respond to invoke the desired results you want. Just remember, it may not cost you a thing to change your mind but the price for not doing so may cost you a fortune. Nevertheless, your bright future awaits you beyond the turn of these pages having been illuminated with the truth on some of the world's most public secrets to successful living.

NOTES